Bone, Gristle and Fat

poems by

Brian King

Finishing Line Press
Georgetown, Kentucky

Bone, Gristle and Fat

Copyright © 2025 by Brian King
ISBN 979-8-89990-253-6 First Edition
All rights reserved under International and Pan-American Copyright Conventions. No part of this book may be reproduced in any manner whatsoever without written permission from the publisher, except in the case of brief quotations embodied in critical articles and reviews.

ACKNOWLEDGMENTS

The following poems have been previously published in the following journals.

"Hurt", Lingering Between the Margins—a River City Poets Anthology, Joanna Lee, Judy Melchiorre, Marsha Owens Editors, Richmond, Virginia

"Lord Crawdaddy", StreetLight Magazine, Frederick Wilbur, Editor, Charlottesville, Virginia

"Catwalk", Nine Mile Books & Literary Magazine, Robert Herz, Editor, Syracuse, New York

"Autumn—Pas de—Deux", GlassGates Publishing, Megan Konikowski, Editor, Boston Massachusetts

"Autumn—Pas de—Deux", Cortland Standard, Katie Keyser, Editor, Cortland, New York

"Comfort Along Dark Paths", Writing the Land: Virginia (2024) Lis McLoughlin, Editor. Northfield, MA: NatureCulture, LLC

"Life Cycle", Writing the Land: Virginia (2024) Lis McLoughlin, Editor. Northfield, MA: NatureCulture, LLC

Publisher: Leah Huete de Maines
Editor: Christen Kincaid
Cover Art: Brian King
Author Photo: Amy King
Cover Design: Elizabeth Maines McCleavy

Order online: www.finishinglinepress.com
also available on amazon.com

Author inquiries and mail orders:
Finishing Line Press
PO Box 1626
Georgetown, Kentucky 40324
USA

Contents

Gristle
Who Are Your People 1
Mental Mixing Dough Bowl 2
Merit 3
The Others 4
Why Bother 5
Tibetan Mandala 6
Garbage and Treasures Float By 7
All Made One 8
Not Mine Alone 9

Bone
Envelope in White 13
Olly Olly Oxen Free 14
Wind Warm and Blue 15
Members Only 16
Catwalk 17
Seventeen Ninety Nine 19
Mary 20
April at the River 21
Prayer for the Day 22
Angel 23
How Far to Go 24
This is Not Imagined 25
Mom Died on Monday 26

Fat
Autumn Pas de deux 29
Half Moon Bay 30
Cardinal 31
Seasonal 32
Deep Lake 33
Pulling From the Deep 34
Slough 35
Comfort Along Dark Paths 36

Blood
Bird of a Different Feather 39
In a Month 40
The Look of Love 41
Hurt 42
Greater Awareness 43
An Open Window is More Than a Metaphor 44
Affirmation 45

Muscle
Our Name Isn't Kennedy 49
Trading Vices, Tears 50
Briars, Brambles and Thorns 51
I Heart Jesus 52
Leave 53
No Clown 54

Flesh
Semisweet Defeat 57
Find Yourself 59
New Years Eve Nashville 1977 60
Lordy Crawdaddy 61
Well Hello There 62
Orange Slices 64
The Government Cheese 65
Life Cycle 67

About the Author 69

Dedicated to Amy

Gristle

Who Are Your People

Looks like an oak, maybe a beech's brown leaf,
possibly six inches long, possessing a different energy
months ago.

Today acrid grey smoke wafts from the hill,
a house fire? no; a scofflaw burns
leaves in his front yard.

See him laughing as a swath of yellow flames
surround the trees, crunchy oak leaves releasing
stored carbon and heat.

He's getting away with this—here, today!
You my friend are not from these parts.
Who are your people?

When I was young our neighbors piled
maple and oak leaves in tiny backyards,
lit afternoon fires, casually smoked cigars.

Brisk autumn winds swept grey smoke over blocks
of starter homes during the day while industry's
black ash covered laundry on the clothes line.

We inhaled too much smoke, washed the ash
from our clothes, this was our lot, never asking
where we belonged.

Mental Mixing Dough Bowl

Millennial men wearing aviators,
  women with RayBans;
    I assume they're human.

I'm concerned when
 I see the sunglass flock:
  sunglasses worn on a cloudy day,
    tinted eyeballs hiding something.

They move with confident indifference.
 I want to stop them,
   ask them to remove those
     dark eyeshades,
       stop their retreat.

Was I asking too much?
 just some acknowledgement as a person.
  are we becoming "the other?"

That was my mental mixing bowl of uninformed
 opinion, like a shapeless dough
  of unbaked thoughts, making little sense.

I often fight imaginary dragons,
 fortunately a real encounter with kind and sensitive
  people, wearing RayBans, dispelled my paranoia,
  transforming shapeless dough
    into a baked loaf of rationality.

Merit

Oh merit, I was so young, you presented yourself
in brown drapes, starched white collar and talcum powder,

fragrance found in a jar, a remembrance of
times you smiled, favored and kindled
my naive image of love,

placing me with several others,
new math disciples on television,
demonstrating foreign concepts,

then you set your sights
on someone else, chosen to
sing and dance the latest tunes,

I watched on the sideline
leaving my bereft youth
behind, betrayed.

Oh merit, I retreated into anger,
using my advantage whenever I could,
those times to dominate the unsuspecting

pounce on opportunities, unexplained favors bestowed on me,
often conquering the weak, greed desired more and selfishness
consumed my mind,

sidetracked often by an ego that wouldn't let go
of fairness, what is fair? the war, violence on the
children.

Oh merit, we mistake and falsify the reality of avarice,
winner takes all and that's never enough.

The Others

It's easy to formulate and theorize,
imagining myself as that pretty good guy
until

the unexpected appears
often in the form of a stranger's looks or behavior.
so it is when my silly inconvenience began;

her cart had 17 items not the required 10—I almost say something,
someone ahead of her tries to buy beer without money or proper ID—
    ridiculous,
the final straw is the guy buying a 2 liter soda—lacking the necessary
    money,

all of us make it through the line, are on our way,
intersecting in a grocery store. How were they allowed in
my place of space, rules, money?

I return safely to my hilltop home
away from those people, them—
their actions ingrained in my memory as odd.

It came to me later—I need to be with them longer
than those few minutes
experiencing what they lack

I often fail to fulfill accepted notions of propriety,
stumbling bumbling my way, inconveniencing someone,
becoming an annoyance,
that's when I'll join the others.

Why Bother

What is the purpose of seeing every potential,
all the pieces,
do we win a prize,
are we ever fulfilled by this game?

I don't delight in mystery, sometimes I'm afraid,
today there is a gentle reminder of the big world.

I look out my window at the forest,
through the distance of mist I see a lone branch silhouetted by the
    morning sun
framed in place from the tall oaks and their leaves,
each bird has a distinct song and calls out
they seem happy.

I join them, watching and hearing the world.
I learn not to care about the grand plan today:
fret not hairy big brain apeman
become quiet like these little ones
you are better off knowing peace
than reaching for a shadow.

Tibetan Mandala

Out of the corner of my eye I watch the monks complete the mandala.
what emerges is a new dimensional existence,
a prism keeps the colors apart, my eye sees each grain of sand
contributing to the tableau with their gods' healing.
The mandala is complex, yet watch it dissolve into a pile,
sweeping that intricate structure into the urn.

I think of
my ending,
a mixture of colors
devolving into tissue, blood, water,
now bone, eventually merged with earth.

At least the mandala goes to a river,
merges with the water and becomes one with the earth.
Maybe cremation isn't a bad thing,
just wondering if there will be a reassembly in the future,
into a facsimile of what I was.

Garbage and Treasures Float By

In the river of experience
a man made of mesh jumps in,
all chicken wire silvery thin,
his little barbs of steel gathering
everything floating by.

Using thoughts like food—images as sustenance,
they lap against his mind,
soft imprints in the sand of consciousness
bent over analyzing every item,
the mesh man stays aloof, above it all.

He ventures out in the world
looking for relationships not in his programming.
Beyond data, facts, analysis,
there's a constant uneasiness,
he knows something else is there.

Once he was told to have faith,
what he sought appeared,
not knowing what it was he discarded the thing
and went on,
oblivious.

All Made One

No one is with you,
last images, voices,
gasps of breath, no
more, this ending.

You're number one or one million
it's inconsequential.

All are gathered
without fanfare.
Jewelry removed,
bodies prepped,
transferred to cardboard boxes.
you lie together,
a community of sorts.

The assembly line moves
to the furnace,
silently progressing into
the flames,
two hours elapse.

All remains are ground.
Like fine coffee,
ash transferred to fifty five gallon
drums, labelled by date
of death.

Outside the facility, a communion
of sorts, is available for the survivors.
One five hundred milliliter bag contains
an aggregate
of lives dispensed,
then disposed.

Not Mine Alone

I look out at nearly naked branches of
six tall oaks sixty feet away,
yellow leaves weave and spin
hanging with their small stems, spindles of wood.

It is enough that I watch, catalog them,
a luxury of admiring the elegance of movement,
experiencing autumn in peace.

One step further—I'll put this idea on the page, send it out.
Does it really matter?

There's the possibility of sharing words,
going out into the unknown,
someone may need them.

Bone

Envelope in White

Anticipating joy, I see the star magnolia tree,
those white flowers are the first to come out in early March.
Like you they brighten our world, delicate and lovely.

Wrapping you in my arms we walk this mile,
with each step floppy petals multiply on our path,
softening the frozen grey asphalt.

I stand looking through a canopy to a clear sky
and feel future possibilities,
not only when these white stars blossom
on this day, but every day.

Olly Olly Oxen Free

I'd like to dance, hold you tight, look into your eyes and
you, look into mine.
I want to dance, not tripping on my words, glances or touch,
a memory to hold on to,
it could mean so much.

She said "remember that day
when you stepped out,
not on yourself
or me.
you have a lot to offer
don't be afraid I won't hurt you."

I said "thank you,
I wish I could
cause there's something inside
that's afraid if I do."

Make the leap. Take the step.
Risk a chance. Unbind that chain.

Everybody, everybody out!
Olly Olly oxen free.

Wind Warm and Blue

A few days ago it was bright and warm
I walked outside and immediately felt the connection,
the wind, trees, leaves fluttering with rhythm.

See the mud flats,
wonderful scales of chocolate curled up in the sun,
memories from childhood: picking at the dirt,
gingerly avoiding the slick, sticky parts.
Now that is fun.

I might be back,
the nut on the side of the road,
a man child.

Members Only

Something startles me
out of the stupor,
predicting a future state,
a place in eternity,

reservations aren't required,
come as you are
everything is provided,
it's an all inclusive resort.

When I drop my requirement to exist
doors open
the path is evident,
faith fuels the journey onward.

I'd like to leave my baggage at the train station,
it might take a celestial travel agent,
but everything is done online now by machines
and they aren't very reassuring.

I look at the sky, the sun and stare at a fig tree
feel free,
connected to the present
and earthly dust.

Catwalk

I walk from open grass fields into
the amalgam of glass and concrete,
obscuring sky with sharp angles,
vacant buildings, until the slender

brown footpath through
pawpaw trees and poke leads
me past rushing canal waters
down a ladder, ten feet to silver

steel and iron bars. A two foot wide
grid extends like a mirage into the distance
above a forty inch diameter
metallic colon, flushing waste
somewhere down river.

I stroll lazily beneath
iron black arches creating optical illusions,
train tracks from mountains headed to the sea,
creosote's odor, coal train's screeching
wheels overhead. Watch buzzards circle.

It is Sunday or any day of the week,
the scene is the same along the pipeline,
look left, wild life—five men, river sand in their hair,
glazed eyes, some unconscious, but
I am not a ghost, keep walking turning my back to
strange men with pony tails and women whose
weak perfume mingles with southern breezes.

The catwalk ends,
lowers me to boulders of cinnamon
and chocolate, hollows carved slowly
by liquid knives, I climb into clear water.
My feet slip on the silt, one foot too far
I'm swept under rapids.

For a few seconds I lose my fear of death,
my body cools, my heart doesn't stop beating,
I emerge under azure skies, green trees,
the white sun blazes.

Seventeen Ninety Nine

At one of many suburban strip malls;
a clerk informs shoppers:
"those art supplies aren't included in the two for one deal."

The twelve by sixteen inch canvas rests on the floor,
it's seventeen ninety nine, money for gas, lunch, bills, etc.

In one of my many mental worlds a young artist needs, must have,
    requires that canvas,
seventeen ninety nine—*"what's that to me?"*

"I'll pay for it, please take it."
she smiles and asks "what should I paint?".
hesitating I answer "how about a self portrait."

The clerk's prattle:
"how nice, more people should do that, our society is in trouble",
ill at ease, I ask myself *"is this just cheap grace?"*

Close by at another obsolete suburban mall;
Barnes and Noble has a seventeen ninety nine poetry collection
I don't need, require, depend upon,
but I want it.

In my car,
looking upward—a conflagration of seagulls and cumulus wind swept
    wonderment.
I'm overtaken unexpectedly with sadness as tears well up.

Dad's whisper through spirit worlds,
"an artist needs supplies, here's one hundred and twenty dollars."

Mary

She earned an advanced philosophy degree,
took vows of silence, poverty, chastity,
then a religious calling—off to the Canadian wilds,
sequestered to live in silence and serve the Indigenous people.

At the communal dinner table I listen intently; her current career:
helping integrate the mentally ill into society.
Mary looks at me, serenely.
She asks "What do you do?"

I'm out of my element here.
With nervous chatter, fumbling for words—
"Uh, I work for one of the largest defense contractors in the country."
In this moment where minutes seem like hours, I continue,
"We make things which kill large numbers of people, more effectively:
drones, fighter jets, lasers, bombs, all that stuff.
I mean I don't make them, or kill people,
I just work for the company and they have people that do that.
I'm a computer systems architect on a multi billion dollar IT contract.
Then there's the money, you know, the money?"
Do I work just for the money?
And that ends our dinner conversation.

During the day I see her swimming the crawl in the cool Adirondack
lake, we never speak with each other again.

April at the River

I want to run fast and jump high,
it wasn't to be,
instead the challenge—lifting myself up to the sky,
there are no beanstalks.

It's not easy climbing the magic vine at the river.
The twisted chocolate roots, solid paper strips,
hold me as I go up, sit waiting for prey.

I am the tiger, hidden in the tree, shadowed with the evening's light.
My shadow mistaken for a dogwood.
Another passerby walks below
ignoring the silly man in the tree,
clinging to the chocolate roots.

"What you doing up there mister?"
Growing tired, bored.

Back down.
Thump to the soft earth.
Neither tiger, or dogwood,
just trying to capture youth and play
down by the river in April.

Prayer For The Day

In the morning I try
to reconcile the worries of yesterday,
today and tomorrow.

My grip weakens.
I pray to God for favors—
"release my unrealistic expectations."

From the foggy experience—clarity,
the light of dawn,
a voice, vision, thought, from
The One: *"I did this, you didn't and can't."*

Peace arrives,
the sun rises again, I breathe,
feel my body come alive,
the heaviness lifts.

I live here and needn't be
the caretaker of the world.
Remember to be thankful:
son, brother, husband, father
and friend.

Angel

Yes you are connected to an angel

transfixed by an apparition, in the wide blue expanse,

she speaks a language we all understand:

"I don't appear often, I join with you when celestial and earth merge,

you are precious, unique,

our spirits are one, the pure and the fair, holding on,

it is a time of transcendence, nourishment for your soul,

your journey."

How Far to Go

My blue umbrella looks out on the trees,
thinking about Mom,
I'd like to be closer to good memories,
not the ones of the ending
those are important,
I'd rather they not dominate my memory.

Am I fooling myself,
a long trip to see Dad
thinking we'll be brought closer,
or the memories will be better once he's gone
I hope.

Do we live this life only once?
It's not clear,
there's gnawing, a need to know

it's hard to believe darkness is acceptable,
trying to build a fire isn't easy,
cultivating an inner flame.

This is Not Imagined

My Mother has fallen I
>run to her,
>pull her up from the floor,
>clothe her nakedness,
>carry her to the couch.

My Heart is heavy
She lays down sadly aware of how weak she is,
I hold her
"It's alright Mom."
She closes her eyes, falls asleep I
>stay with Mom during the night,
>listen to Mom asking for water,
>hear Mom talking—a drug induced speech about her dead brother Jimmy,
>sleep, wake, sleep, administer morphine,
>ponder life,
>pray for you Mom.

Cancer
>You tricky mother fucker,
>one year wreaking havoc,
>remission for four years,
>one year taking a breast,
>another four year remission,
>then it ends.

Mom Died on Monday

Monday morning my sister calls,
left a message to call her,
I call back,
at least they were with her.

Thought I'd get up that Friday, but I was too late,
forty thousand miles driving back and forth,
funeral is Friday,
time for my eulogy,
glad I practiced.

I walk outside to her memorial,
magnolias' sweet smell drifts over long blades of green grass,
a late afternoon sun bakes the sandstone and my skin in 90 degree heat.

Squinting I remember,
a blue heron gliding over the pond,
Her soul and spirit released from cancer.

Today an army of men cut grass in tennis ball yellow vests, sunglasses
    and floppy hats,
the pine siskin are somehow related to these guys,
just as Amy and I are a pair of bluebirds on the telephone wire,
the cardinal looks in the window,
Mom are you there?

Fat

Autumn Pas de deux

Chestnut, white oak and poplar frame a southwestern sky,
their summer leaves mingle with ten knot westerly winds.
Thus begins—a slow shaking of leaves, dancers waving.

Imperceptibly leaves change color,
thirst, grow brittle,
and the wind—never enough to tear limb from trunk—
caresses each one; asking "how does this feel?"

Leaves—"empty yourself while touching, listen."

Wind—"I see, getting closer I hear!"

Winds increase, lifts leaves, with a whirl
and shake, snap, they are free.

Move up, side to side, circle, thrust, tumble

a final repose absorbs leaves back to Earth
while the wind turns its back and heads east.

Half Moon Bay

There's the Cisco awards banquet tonight,
        yet with a day to myself I
leave San Francisco after lunch, drive I-280,
        over the Santa Cruz mountains,
through redwood forests, past artichoke farms,
        strawberry farm stands.

I enter Half Moon Bay.
        The narrow road leads to sand, tall grasses,
Pacific Ocean.
        No East Coast beach blight.

Roll up the gabardine trousers,
        remove my black cap toes,
knee socks, walk on a mixture of dark brown sugar
        and gravel, there's a worn rock of basalt, sit,
watch the vast blue gray water, listen
        slight thunder-of breakers, iridescent
feet slide in a foot of surf.

        Her soft voice like ocean's breeze,
gentle, she offers grapes, green and clean
        they're just grapes,

experiencing unexpected feelings,
        a scene out of a late sixties movie?
my West Coast first.

        What's out here?
I like this slipping into paradise,
        the kindness of strangers,
an ease of existence.

Cardinal

You got my attention today crimson,
sitting up in the monochromatic tangle
of brush, branches and shrubs,
the metaphor hits me immediately,
I won't deny the beauty of a red bird,
I can't.

How can I explain it away?

Which leads me to the Divine,
why can't it exist amidst the mundane sameness of humanity,
we can't refute the red bird's loveliness.

Disbelief in the Divine is serious stuff.
Better to rationalize and cut it all down
so only the stubble and dry parched earth remain,
still the bird flies.

Seasonal

Autumn arrives—shorter days, gray skies, cool breezes,
I wish for light, it melts away,
curtains close, dust settles.

Farewell sunflowers say your last goodbye,
husks in sun scorched heaps lie withered,
colors melting away to amber.

Nowhere for the goldfinches to land and fill their hunger,
acrobatic songsters effortlessly rise then fall on tepid currents.
Swallowtail butterflies take their place now,
eleven crossing the continent this year.

The transformation of tall sunflower now laid low,
becoming food for beetles, flies and worms,
I'm a perennial being, more than a year's cycle.

Deep Lake

Be a lake
a deep lake
absorbing, reflecting,
dancing with sun, the wind.

I need flow
keeping stagnation away.

From above
a stream of grace
comes,

it's difficult to be in contact
when feelings and thoughts are in the depths
not hiding, just not obvious.

Oh be a lake
a deep lake

there's a limit to the amount of dirt I can clean
it takes time to muddy the waters and clean up
my waves are high and hurt
it takes so much sun to warm me up.

I still like the idea of a big lake
a deep lake.

Pulling From the Deep

Funny how you can catch a fish by throwing a small fish
into the water.
Water that you don't know much about
the depth or what's underneath.
You have some intuition and hope that there is a hungry fish
willing to take your bait.
It strikes and you have a bit of a struggle, but most times you win the
battle and are happy to
see this foreigner emerge from their home.
Why then is it so different to go down into the
heart, mind, subconscious?
You'd think the owner would know more than they do
about themselves.
The things that come out in dreams, what we say, or express,
oh how they seem like that foreigner we pulled out of the water
writhing and trying to get away back home.
There is fatigue, a bit of pain
examining what we've found
confounds.
Time to fish again in the murky depths of our souls.

Slough

Between a leg of green grass with moss and a rocky thigh lies a deep
slough of river water. Dead river birch, poplar and sycamore trees
dam the flow.

It's that muddy water dividing two strands
which captures my eye. The river runs too fast, so
I slip off my clothes among arrow root and fiddle heads,
launch my mind and body in coffee foam liquid.

Luxurious mud, river sand, silt covers my furry legs and arms,
the skin soothed, baths of brown goo.

I should take the river's course for a cleansing, mind is full of anxious
memories and tomorrow's worries—too much time wallowing in the
slough, the accumulation of past misadventures piles up like the logs
    holding fast.
when the dam breaks I'll be free.

Comfort Along Dark Paths

Find a quick path
to Ware Creek,
thick blankets of pine needles
cushion my feet,

precise arrangements of pins on the ground,
what formula is this?
an equation, any symbolism?

Gravity and the downward gentle angle
keeps me going,
the creek is close, can't be far,
deceptively close.

I choose narrow trails barely recognizable,
free to follow the slope and gullies
lead me along ridges to

a sacred space:
sixty foot trees, a spirit shelter
of
mountain laurel,
ferns, mosses
rising from pine and oak paths.

I rest and scan the woods without concern
no reason to leave this fertile enclave,
shadows lengthen. I desire a deep sleep
on the bed of green moss blankets.

Inner peace ignites,
belonging and tranquility,
then the inevitable shift
better be going,
stand up and walk away,
take these lasting impressions
and form a different reality
with gratitude.

Blood

Bird of a Different Feather

Effortlessly he navigates main street on a
lamplighter bicycle: high heels,
pink and orange polkadot blouse
clashing with the blue, green and white striped
mini-skirt. At least the gold bracelets are tastefully
arrayed on slim arms and sleek legs.
I wouldn't have chosen the black cowboy hat
for summer wear, maybe a cream panama.

I sit with Amy under crepe myrtle's shade,
a spicy bloody mary, shrimp and creamy cheese grits
arrive. Our bike rider is playing summer hits
from the seventies. He's been parading in this town
for decades, his lovely movements of torso and arms
remind me of herons lifting from the water.

In a Month

A gift; another month observing
Earth's and Moon's transit: east to west,
contemplating celestial patterns.

Look east, a full moon rises over the trees,
ribbons of luminescence bisect the river,
clear water rolls through tumbled granite,
a cadence lulls me towards sanguine sleep.

Eventually we return to rocky banks, clamber up
in darkness, scan the sky,
absorb the pleasures of this night,

between a push pull of
love and fear, wholeness, slivers of commonality
there's never a steady tide

but, here I am, sitting next to you,
as it was twenty eight days ago,
sharing this passing moment.

The Look of Love

Dear friend
where have you been all these years?
I hear your voice
and with my eyes behold your presence
I reach out, you reach back,
we embrace
our eyes gaze deeply into each other,
we are no longer apart
but one.
It shakes me
witnessing the recognition between two beings,
assuming one superior to the other,
realize
love brings us together
despite so many differences there is
an opening
where love flows in
and out
years separate you from me,
I believe
differences and distances are bridged
not by knowledge
but by love.

Hurt

You must have been in pain while you harvested your garden knowing

You would be the one to stop the growth
of something so wonderful, beautiful and a gift to many,
and it was of your self, heart, sweat and toil that helped nurture this
wonderful landscape.

They'll never know how much it means to you,
I have some insight, yet I wasn't the one who created the masterpiece
and you dearest are hurt.

I won't forget the sight of you: hoe, rake and wheel barrow carrying
something you loved down to the woods where they'll rest and return to
our Creator.

Greater Awareness

I had a dream
that I knew you
and you knew me

then I realized I didn't
know me or you.

Bogged down with imprints from the past you didn't create
I carry them with me
pulling out

the sword from its sheath
steel on steel
cutting and slashing

I see blood
ours
the gurgling wound oozing

escaping now
weakness

oh yes now
for once I see the parallels
clashing

it is time to disengage
and face a truer realism

that I had a dream
I knew
you and me,
I now know.

An Open Window is More Than a Metaphor

The car windows are open.
>It won't rain.
>I'll leave them down.

The car windows are open.
>It will rain.
>I get the keys, open the door and sit,

sometimes in silence.
Starting the engine—I roll them up.

Again—the windows are down.
>Why?
>It could be as simple as the air conditioning isn't working.

Maybe you like the breeze, the fresh air of an open window?
>I suppose so, never thought of that before.

This really isn't about car windows, is it?
>No it isn't,
>relax.
>I'll let the windows down
>and be better for it.

Affirmation

My feet ache
the heat of the day steals my strength

I know you are here
by my side

still there are
chest pains, my mind plays tricks,

I feel worn and old
yet happiness ensues

we continue our walk together
knowing we spent many years together,

on this burning hot summer Sunday
my love for you is all that matters.

Muscle

Our Name Isn't Kennedy

"I choose to write poems in this decade and do the other things, not because they are factual, but because they are fictitious"

In a photo from Easter 1964 my sister Barbara wears a bright yellow wool
coat, a child's fedora indicates the serious task awaiting me,
groomed for a role I never asked for.
Starched white shirt, school tie and leather solicitor's briefcase added to
the pain of great expectations.

John Fitzgerald Kennedy come back.

In an attempt to bring back the myth of Camelot, we
are exposed to Kennedy lore: PT-109, Marilyn Monroe, Hyannis,
Bay of Pigs, the Cuban Missile Crisis.

Four long journeys to Hyannis,
standing at the Kennedy compound wall,
glimpses of sacred grounds
radiating the privilege of a wealthy bootlegger.

We knelt at Our Lady of Victory Catholic Church,
the same church Rose Kennedy attended. Eyes on
the crucified Lord and side glances toward the gods
they wished
we were.

Ahh childhood—at least we went on vacations,

had clean clothes
&
food on the table.

Trading Vices for Tears

I visit the land of medical machinations,
the nurse exclaims: "results aren't good,
 99% shows total infiltration of the arteries, don't panic"
Don't panic—really!

Don't take me now.

I'll change, I swear.

What must go, what remains?
choices.

"Hello—You there?"
Through the telephone I hear your trembling voice,
imagine precious tears.

I'll trade my vices for your tears,
the battle with addiction continues.

Briars, Brambles and Thorns

Bothersome questions
from a large and close extended family—

"Oh, BK, your face looks so much better."
    "Thanks Aunt Shirley."
        Severe acne hit my senior year of high school,
        I have enough problems with self esteem.

"Do you have a girlfriend?"
    "No I don't."
        Trying, everybody, really trying.
        No, I want to be alone the rest of my life.

"What are you studying?"
    "Mathematics."
        The fewest degree requirements getting me out of this
        fucking place sooner.

"What do you want to do after college?"
    "I'm undecided."
        If I can play guitar and drink with my friends that's
        enough.

"Oh you could be an accountant."
    "No, Grandma, I don't want to be an accountant."
        I don't want to be working
        in an office—43 years later that's still true.

I Heart Jesus

I Heart Jesus—a bumper sticker on a small white SUV keeping pace, I-95,
normally I dial up a distaste for bumper sticker theology
judging the owners as foolish or judgmental.

This day is different,
I admire the innocence, the profession of love
this proclamation is authentic, joyful

would I place I heart Jesus stickers on my car for everyone to see?
Would I be lying if I did?
I'm happy to see this simple statement

there's no self righteousness
no theological bullying
no condemnation or judgment

in a small metal box riding on the dangerous highway,
thank you for simplicity, earnestness
three words made an impact.

Leave

Expiration date
August seventeen two thousand eighteen
leave corporate hive

the promise of something better
end of my era,
year after year of semi-appreciated sameness, toil,
drudgery, three decades collapse into one hour.

There's no path going back,

I can't predict what is coming.

Saddle off the old horse, there's a new horse to ride.

New routines, new challenges
once friends, now they're social media posts
then obituaries.
Find my way from there, to now and then—whatever.

No Clown

Look in the mirror,
a forty seven year memory
putting thick white paste on my face,
my patchwork beard was red and curly.

What a year that was; digging out of an academic hole,
wasted time drinking, violent anger, despair,
searching for some self esteem;
I volunteer for a silly college function, be a clown for some local kids.

Early Saturday morning in February is cold.
Should have slept in past noon. Some false notion of
redemption kept me going. Turned on the radio,
heard another maudlin song, Leo Sayer, I tried relating to.

Walking across snow, wearing pajamas, the silent campus grounds,
no one up yet.
At the elementary school I participate in some games,
quickly realize my presence was not required,
the kids were cruel, mean spirited.
Time's up, get out, I don't belong and no one cares.

Somehow it's seemed alright,
justifying repeated intoxication, anger, guilt and remorse.
It took years to get beyond that phase.
I am transformed now,
I'm no clown.

Flesh

Semisweet Defeat

Never thought we'd be friends; Billy can't believe
I have thirty-four dollar Adidas Titans,
red suede shoes—beautiful.
Wealthy kid competing against a country boy.
Athletes struggle, running, farther, faster—
bonds form despite our differences.

Coach Luke decides we'll run the novice mile:
Manley Field House, The Hill, SU basketball's arena, biggest
indoor invitational track meet of the winter. Five hundred elite
athletes from upstate New York compete on
the wooden oval,
eleven laps to a mile.
Spring in those boards, should be an easy race, prove
to ourselves—winners.

Starting gun fires. Runners pound the boards, cadence of the swift
reverberates off the walls in the old field house.
Unwillingly—Billy and I are running against the best milers in the state,
Coach—why are we here?

Maybe it isn't a mistake—
Coach Luke's stories—invading Italy, Anzio beach, pinned
down by Nazi guns, slaughter, terror,
never make it out alive—then living, he's never the same.
Luke's motivations, morality, resonance is wasted on us,
he survived the Depression, the War.
Rich suburban kids are soft.

Started too fast,
passed by the leaders after 6 laps!
Meet Officials yell at us—
"You—move—move to the outer lane!"
Is this really happening?

The winner, super fast, finishes in four minutes twenty-five seconds.
Hear the echoes of our plodding strides on the wood—
thump thump, dah dah dah, dumb.
Stretching out forever—cross the finish line

one minute later.
It's over—
run into the bowels of Manley—hide,
Coach Luke's silence, in humility
we taste Anzio beach.

Find Yourself

Before this I've never been further west than Rochester,
the East confines, rules abound,
the West is where I'll find authentic purpose,

I spend thirty-one hours sitting against this bus window,
a vast Texas landscape unfolds, wheels in constant
low pitched reverberation. My companion:
Leon Uris's Trinity, no idea when I'll eat or find a real bathroom.
With little sleep, body aches, my head hurts.

Fort Worth, Waco,
Abilene, Amarillo, Lubbock,
Raton, on and on to the mile high city,

Getting together after a long break
with my old college roommate Kelly.

We were close a few years ago, mistaken at
times for each other: two bearded Upstate
hard drinking pranksters.

Time reveals our differences,
after two years we move 180 degrees apart,
go to different places in life.

He's working a computer job—oil exploration, corporate
benefits, health insurance, adult shit, girlfriend, his own apartment,
drives a nice Triumph Spitfire convertible.

I'm on the last lap of the undergraduate
rat race wondering what I've been missing out
on. Maybe Kelly got it right.

Exhausted, I call, pay phone from the Greyhound
station, he arrives—*nice car Kelly, but I need food and sleep.*

New Years Eve Nashville 1977

A green Cadillac picks us up.
Two older guys looking like Charlie Daniels
drink Jack and we smoke weed—
a mistake: the paranoia, the "I-might-die-tonight"
reckless driving on route 40
through these East Tennessee mountains.

We're helpless in the back. These guys have guns,
but they're headed for Nashville so we stay,
exiting at the famous Gruen's guitar store,
where the guys want to party, but we say, "No, friends,
thanks for the ride" and find another five-dollar hotel.

Tin Pan Alley dinner, then a Clint Eastwood flick,
the theatre is a good place to wind down before
visiting the Grand Hyatt Hotel sky deck's big formal party—
Leisure suits, bouffant hair, ball gowns.
"What in the cornbread hell are you two
long-haired bearded vagrants doing here?"

Yet, we're calling ourselves college geniuses—the observation
deck is a prime spot to take in the Nashville lights,
when out of the cold, three white security guards appear,
and we're manhandled down the snarling stairs.

Lordy Crawdaddy

On highway 10–high risk—no space to fall.
Cars come so close at high speeds,
their wind moves us in the wrong direction.
On the entrance ramp, there's
8 inches of clearance between the wall
and the road to Baton Rouge.

The white Dodge Dart pulls over.
An old man: "You want a ride? get in."
He stares ahead, a stone.
Sharp and I sit next to him in the front bench seat —
the man's hands! Each finger tattooed
letters spelling Hard Luck Lost Love—
no questions from me.
"Do you drink beer?"
damn tired, hungover from New Orleans,
I babble "Uh, yes. Sometimes I do and sometimes I don't;
it depends."
"Goddammit! I asked, do you drink beer?"
I'm yelling, Sharp's yelling
"Yes sir. Yes, sir we drink beer."
"Reach behind that cooler, get us 3.
Don't let anyone see I got to get to Seattle—
I don't have no driver's license or registration."
I reach into the styrofoam cooler
grab 3 Dixie beers. We drink.

He pulls off the side of the highway.
"I got to take me a piss."
Tall rushes provide cover.
The old man's got the hood of the car open,
He's pissing into the radiator.
An hour goes by, driving west on route 10, we break.
I'm eating a hot roast beef sandwich, nice—-
gravy and mashed potatoes.
We think we've made a new friend,
but he matter-of-fact delivers his goodbye:
"I'm done with you; you're on your own."

Well Hello There

> As the back of her SUV opens at Trader Joes,
> I witness a vinyl blowup doll with an erection,
> maybe he's a comfort companion, party gift or pleasure item?

These dolls are designed and advertised for sexual stimulation, companionship, artistic representations of human fantasy, and other creative pursuits, such as photography.

> Conversation with my Father at Shopper's Fair, 1965—"No Dad—GI Joe isn't a doll, he's an action figure!"

Sex doll-owners are members of a marginalized population, and accessing the population is challenging as many members of the community wish to remain anonymous for fear of judgment, persecution, and psychiatric labeling.

> Popular tune marketing the product in 1965 "GI Joe, GI Joe fighting man from head to toe, on the land, on the sea, in the air."—to the tune Over There—

Although the primary function of these dolls is ostensibly sexual in nature, doll-owners have described varying levels of emotional attachment to their sex dolls, from identification of their doll as a life partner, to describing their doll as a mere novelty item.

> Justification—"GI Joe, he's a Marine, I bought him with my allowance."

Accounts of Agalmatophilia, the pathological condition in which some people establish exclusive sexual relationships with statues, dates back to ancient Greece (Scobie & Taylor, 1975).

> One child's toy is another's fantasy object—I find my GI Joe naked, wrapped in electrical tape under my younger brother's bed.

Nonetheless, there has been no investigation into whether consumers of the modern sex doll are mentally or emotionally disturbed. Neither has there been a professional discussion regarding the modern day equivalent of Agalmatophilia as a diagnosable and treatable condition.

    She sees me looking at her and the doll, she turns him over—protecting something—I avert my gaze.

Agalmatophilia is not to be confused with the fictional and supernatural powers of those who bring a statue to life, referred to as Pygmalionism (Scobie & Taylor, 1975).
According to Ovid's Metamorphoses, book X, Pygmalion was a misogynist who sculpted a perfect woman out of ivory.

Orange Slices

Mindlessly eating my Veggie-Max sandwich,
sitting at the East Coast
Subway on route 10 Chester, Virginia
I realize they have the best retro candy on display:
peach slices, orange peanuts and gummy bears.

My eyes search all over, can't find those orange slices!
Below the gold glittered display shelf
a treasure box contains Binney & Smith crayons,
Duncan yo-yos, Silly Putty, a Slinky.

A $19.99 deal, sixty years of childhood memories:
    silly putty was off limits in our house,
    we were denied the fun, stretching faces of
    colorful comic characters, Mom "heard"
    it ruins the upholstery.
Another memory gateway back.

There's always time to buy Necco Wafers, Black Jack gum,
but no orange slices.

The Government Cheese

The big adventure and step forward was grinding to a halt,
money,
it takes money to fuel the dream
no matter how obscure.

I put my faith in the government institution only to be told
Reagan done eliminated student aid.
My fuel for the year—dried up.

Reincarnated as a coyote I found various ways of surviving,
fences of poverty were keeping me hungry, running always looking.

Thanks to crippling inflation and a recession opportunities were
abundant
if you knew where to look.

First stop the Virginia unemployment agency.
Each week I rode the ten speed down and waited with the others
wasting half a day to have my paper work
reviewed and approved by the human robots.
Miserable disdain on their countenance
yet noncompliance forfeits the $250.

Emergency food stamps,
a nice pickup for another week.
Yes Ukrops I am buying this prime rib with the government money.

My senses were always on alert looking for more food
in bold type
One day only—Richmond Arena
Free cheese and butter to the needy.

The great leveler—poverty and hunger.
I wait in the procession of fellow down and outers
urban hobos.
In the future they'll fight over fifty dollar laptops.

Entering the dark space of the arena
I finally claim my prize,
surplus butter and the unusually large yellow rectangle
5lbs of a food like substance
labeled cheese,
neither cheddar—oh the beautiful black diamond cheddar it was not,
nor the sublime Stilton?

You my prize go in the backpack and I ride off on ten-speed.
Yes my dear here is our bounty,
we have descended
into the ranks of the poor
and hungry
eating from the government cheese.

Government cheese you're one of many icons;
time transformed me into a coyote
scrounging for a meal
searching for sustenance when the ego was crushed
a small cinder ready to expire.

Life Cycle

Long walk down to the field,
it's easier in December than in the heat of June.
The view: large rectangles of bright cerulean
sky, rows of brown earth framed by the evergreen,

so many pine rows hint at the history
of loblolly cut and processed upriver for pulp.
There's an industrial manmade feel to these woods.

I come at this hour to sit in a fallow field,
watch for deer, the sky for migrating fowl,
listen—chickadees and the gold finches
searching among the dried remains
for food.

Reclining in the sun,
a broken stalk, the dead sunflower,
its seven inch diameter head,
threadbare, swaying in wind of five knots,
the weight of its head bowing to a ground that sprouts dandelions.

I grasp the head,
pinch, rub and release fluff, fuzz and black seeds,
separate the edibles, chew, swallow
relish the gift of this small black entity.
Not just food, but a testament to continuation,
a possibility of new growth.

Brian King read *John Welch, O.Carm.'s Spiritual Pilgrims: Carl Jung and Teresa of Avila* in the summer of 2012. Jung's ideas sparked a desire in him to explore emotions, memories, and society in the form of short poems. He joined River City Poets of Richmond, participating in critique groups and public readings. He writes from his experience as the oldest in a family of seven, a truck driver, a laboratory technician at a chlorine chemical factory, an art gallery employee, and a retired IT professional with 33 years of experience. He rode motorcycles in his youth and hitchhiked through the Deep South. With a B.A. in Mathematics from Albany University and a Master of Fine Arts in painting from Virginia Commonwealth University, he brings a unique background to poetry. Raised in Syracuse, New York, he has lived in Richmond, Virginia, since 1982. He is a husband, father, and grandfather.

This collection of poems owes much to the support of friends, teachers, and mentors: Joanna Lee, Poet Laureate of Richmond and president of River City Poets; John Cherenzia of Café Zata; Leslie Shiel and Lauren Miner of Richmond's Visual Arts Center, for their poetry classes and critiques; Father Don Lemay, for planting the seed for writing poetry; Chip Jones, for his continual encouragement; John Vance, for reading the poems and offering thoughtful feedback; Tom England, for his steady support; and Steve McMillan, whose words kept me going through a very dry period of writing.

Most of all, to my wife, Amy—for fifty-seven years of love and unwavering support.

www.ingramcontent.com/pod-product-compliance
Lightning Source LLC
Chambersburg PA
CBHW030057170426
43197CB00010B/1557